Uncommon Traveler
Mary Kingsley in Africa

Written and Illustrated by Don Brown

HOUGHTON MIFFLIN COMPANY
BOSTON

www.houghtonmifflinbooks.com

Calligraphy by Deborah Nadel.
The text of this book is set in Goudy.
The illustrations are pen and ink and watercolor on paper.

Library of Congress Cataloging-in-Publication Data
Brown, Don, 1949–
Uncommon traveler: Mary Kingsley in Africa / written and illustrated by Don Brown.
p.   cm.
Summary: A brief biography of the self-educated nineteenth-century English woman who, after a
secluded childhood and youth, traveled alone through unexplored West Africa in 1893 and 1894
and learned much about the area and its inhabitants.
RNF ISBN 0-618-00273-1   PAP ISBN 0-618-36916-3
1. Kingsley, Mary Henrietta, 1862–1900 — Juvenile literature. 2. Explorers — Africa, West —
Biography — Juvenile literature. 3. Explorers — Great Britain — Biography — Juvenile literature.
4. Woman explorers — Africa, West — Biography — Juvenile literature. 5. Women explorers —
Great Britain — Biography — Juvenile literature. 6. Africa, West — Discovery and exploration
— British — Juvenile literature. [1. Kingsley, Mary Henrietta, 1862–1900. 2. Explorers.
3. Women — Biography. 4. Africa, West — Discovery and exploration.] I. Title.
DT476.23.K56B76   2000
916.604'312'092 — dc21
[B]
99-087823

Manufactured in the United States of America
BVG 10 9 8 7 6 5

For Tyler, an uncommon brother

In 1870, a small house stood on a lonely lane outside London, England.

Bricks filled nearly all of the front windows.
Shutters blocked the back windows.
Vines choked the back wall.
Gloom ruled the rooms.

Eight-year-old Mary Kingsley lived there.

It was as if she lived alone.

Her father, George, traveled the world seeking adventure.
Her mother, also named Mary, was sickly and rarely left her bed.
Her younger brother, Charles, was away at school.

Mary didn't go to school and would never go to school.

"The whole of my childhood and youth was spent at home in the house and garden," she later said. "The living outside world I saw little of. I felt out of place at the few parties I ever had the chance of going to, for I knew nothing of play and such things."

Still, Mary was happy.
"I had a great, amusing world of my own: the books in Father's library."

Novels and poetry books.
Science and history books.
Travel and adventure books.

Books were her companions and teachers.

But there was a life beyond the library, and Mary was a dutiful daughter.

She nursed her mother.

She tidied the house.

She helped her father during his few visits. George Kingsley wrote about his travels, and Mary happily uncovered facts he needed from her beloved library. She knew to be quiet and make little fuss or risk George's temper and have a book thrown at her!

She was the family's handyman, too. Mary taught herself home repair by reading *English Mechanic* magazine.

Once a leaky pipe needed mending.
Standing on a box beneath it, "I cut the lead pipe gallantly through," Mary recalled.
But Mary forgot to turn off the water.
"SWISH came out a jet of water that knocked me over, box and all!"

She had other repairs, other odd jobs, other chores to do. Mary's narrow life as handyman, nursemaid, servant, and aide went on for days, for weeks, for years.

Childhood ended.
Youth disappeared.

In 1892 her mother and father died.
For the first time in her life, good daughter Mary Kingsley was free of her duties.

She was thirty years old.

Her world, once cramped and dark, was now as big as the globe. The idea of it made her head spin.

Inspired by her father's journeys and the travel books she loved, Mary had the remarkable notion of going to West Africa.

People thought Mary was foolish. Much of West Africa was a mystery, even to those who lived there. Visitors risked disease, wild animal attacks, and the hostility of some Africans. West Africa was not a place for a single woman to visit.

Mary ignored the warnings and planned her trip. She would travel light, without a tent, eating native food and wearing her regular English clothes. She would trudge, wade, clamber, and climb in a high-necked, long-sleeved shirt, long heavy skirt, and proper Victorian boots.

She arrived in West Africa in 1893. Mary was delighted. Oh, the grand and vivid sights, sounds, and smells she met!

She ignored the scorching heat and the soggy air.
And the odd insects.

One looked like a "flying lobster." Another, an enormous beetle, flopped into a soup plate
and then shook itself dry "like a retriever."

She collected insects and freshwater fish, which she later donated to the British Museum of
Natural History.

Of course, Mary encountered creatures bigger than fish and insects.

When Mary explored a riverbank, a hippo blocked her way.
"I scratched him behind the ear with my umbrella and we parted on good terms," she said.

In a swamp, an eight-foot-long crocodile "chose to get his front paws over the stern of my canoe." said Mary. "I had to retire to the bow, to keep the balance and fetch him a clip on the snout with a paddle. This was only a pushing young creature who had not learnt manners."

Unfazed by the wild beasts, rough country, and terrific heat, Mary pushed farther inland and met the people who dwelled there.

Once, a trek up a steep hill provided a surprise meeting with some of them.
"I slipped, slid, and finally fell plump through the roof of an unprotected hut," Mary recalled. A great hubbub followed, and she paid for the damage she had done.

Mary met members of the Adjoumba, Igalwa, and M'pongwe tribes, but she felt a special closeness to the Fang people. She admired them greatly.

"The Fang is full of fire, temper, intelligence, and go," she said.

Filled with fire, temper, intelligence, and go herself, Mary was drawn deeper into West Africa.

A paddle wheeler carried Mary more than one hundred miles up the Ogooué River. There she gathered guides and boarded a canoe. The river was treacherous. She and her guides often crashed into boulders or spun wildly in whirlpools and had to leap for their lives.

Mary then plunged into the uncharted forest toward the Remboué River.

It was a wild trek.
The forest canopy hid the sky.
Thick vines roped the trees.
Great blossoms dotted the forest floor in "glorious cups of orange and crimson and pure white."

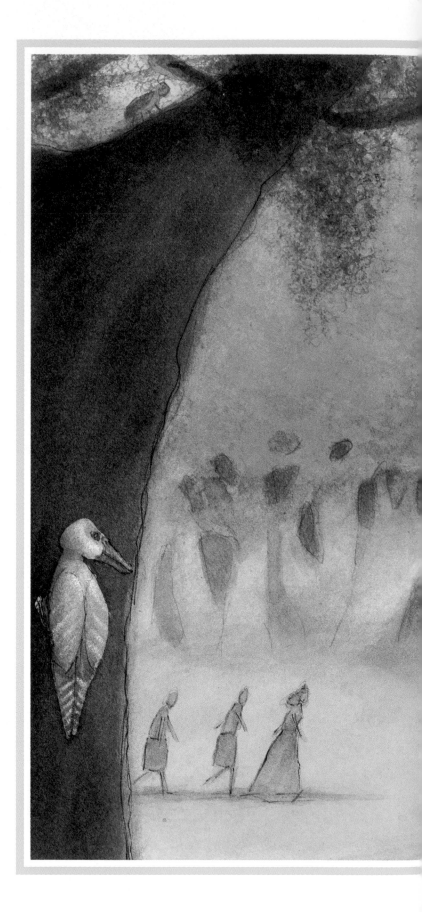

Mary and her guides struggled over a hill covered with broken trees felled by a great storm.
The hot, wet air blanketed them like a great weight.

Elephants, gorillas, and velvety-skinned snakes crossed their path.

They stopped for the night at a Fang village.
Mosquitoes and lice kept Mary awake.
Restless, she borrowed a canoe and slid it into the
nearby lake.

All was purple-black. Only the stars and glowworms
twinkled. Silver-white fish sprang from the water,
reminding Mary of flashing swords.

She paddled to a far bank, stepped onto the shore, and
discovered she wasn't alone.
"I felt the earth quiver under my feet, and heard a soft
big soughing sound, and looking round saw I had
dropped in on a hippo banquet," Mary said. "I made
out five of the immense brutes round me, so I softly
returned to the canoe and shoved off."

She bathed in the lake, returned to camp just before
dawn, and continued on.

Once she stumbled into a spike-filled pit used to trap animals and narrowly escaped harm.
"It is at these times that you realize the blessings of a good thick skirt," she observed.

A slippery log bridged a ravine. Mary walked it like a tightrope.

Mary and her group plodded through sun-cooked swamps of ink-black slime. The stench was awful. Flies pestered them. Sometimes they sank up to their necks in the filthy water.

They finally emerged from the swamps and reached the mud banks of the Remboué River, to the great surprise of nearby villagers. A noisy crowd soon surrounded them.

Mary's journey up the Ogooué River and across the forest to the Remboué River was a great feat, but she didn't crow. She called it a mere "picnic."
Picnic or not, West Africa tugged at Mary.
"If I have a heaven," she said, "that will be mine."

Mary returned to England, where she wrote about Africa and talked about Africa.

Thousands of people read her books and listened to her lectures. They were astonished that a *woman* had experienced such adventures.

She found fame, for which she didn't "care a hairpin."

She still had few friends and felt out of place at parties.

Mary filled her apartment with African masks and charms, baskets and sculptures. She kept the rooms hot and humid.

To remind her of Africa.

To remind her of home.

NOTE

Mary Kingsley was born in England in 1862. By most standards, her childhood was sad and bleak. Her mother was nearly always bedridden. Her father traveled the world as a physician to wealthy patrons, and his infrequent visits home were punctuated with angry outbursts at the normal hubbub of family life. Her brother appears to have been selfish and insensitive.

Young Mary tended to her mother and the household. Though she never went to school, she loved books and learning. How she learned to read is a mystery; it seems she taught herself.

Nevertheless, Mary remembered her childhood fondly. She adored her father. Mary's decision to travel to West Africa was motivated in part by a desire to continue his work; George Kingsley had fancied himself a serious student of foreign cultures.

Uncommon Traveler distills Mary's adventures during her two trips to West Africa in 1893 and 1894. Although she added to knowledge of West Africa, most people were astonished merely by her survival. Supported by her own pluck, Mary flourished in an environment that was often deadly to Africans and non-Africans alike.

Mary's admiration and respect for Africans put her at odds with most of her contemporaries. She felt especially close to people of the Fang (rhymes with *gong*) tribe. Still, it should be noted, she never fully rejected imperialism.

South Africa was her last African destination. There she volunteered to nurse prisoners of the Boer War, caught a fever, and died on June 3, 1900.

Mary Kingsley was thirty-eight years old.

BIBLIOGRAPHY

Frank, Katherine. *A Voyager Out: The Life of Mary Kingsley.* Boston: Houghton Mifflin, 1986.

Gwynn, Stephen. *The Life of Mary Kingsley.* London: Macmillan, 1932.

Kearns, Gerry. "The Imperial Subject: Geography and Travel in the Works of Mary Kingsley and Haford Mackinder." *Transactions of the Institute of British Geographers* 22, no. 4, 1997.

Kingsley, Mary. *Travels in West Africa.* London: Macmillan, 1897.

———. *West African Studies.* London: Macmillan, 1899.